Family Traditions

Italian Roots. American Dreams

writen by **Alessandro Mannino**

illustrated by **Elen Nazaryan**

About the Author

Alessandro was born in the beautiful city of Palermo, Italy. In 2000, when he was just 7 years old, Alessandro moved to the United States with his family. Growing up, he cherished the rich traditions and heritage his family brought with them from Italy. Now, as a father, Alessandro is passionate about passing on these beloved family traditions and the essence of Italian heritage to his own children.

Through the "Italian Roots, American Dreams" series, Alessandro hopes to share the joy and cultural richness of Italian traditions with other Italian American families. These books are crafted with love and care, aiming to create wonderful memories and a strong connection to Italian roots for future generations. Alessandro believes that by celebrating these traditions, families can strengthen their bonds and keep the spirit of Italy alive in their hearts.

Every Sunday, Nico's family gathers for a big dinner.
They eat delicious spaghetti and meatballs made by Nonna.
Nico tries to see how many meatballs
he can stack on his plate without them rolling off.
This tradition is called "La Cena di Domenica."
It brings the family together to share love and laughter.

On special occasions, Nico's family makes pizzelles,
a type of Italian waffle cookie. This tradition, "Fare le Pizzelle,"
is fun because Nico gets to help with the pizzelle iron.
He tries to make the biggest pizzelle ever
and loves tasting the sweet treats
fresh off the press.

On the night before Epiphany,
Nico's family celebrates La Befana.
They leave out stockings for La Befana, a kind old witch
who brings sweets to children.

Nico sneaks a peek and wonders if
La Befana likes chocolate chip cookies as much
as he does. In the morning,
Nico finds his stocking filled with treats!

In March,
Nico's family celebrates the Feast of Saint Joseph.
They make yummy breads and pastries to honor Saint Joseph,
the patron saint of workers and families.
Nico loves the sweet treats and makes funny faces
with the dough before baking!

At Easter,
Nico and his family dye eggs in bright colors.
This tradition is called "La Pasqua."
It celebrates new life and springtime.
Nico always ends up with more dye on his hands
than on the eggs! Nonno tells stories about
Easter parades in Italy
with beautiful costumes.

In the summer,
Nico's town has an Italian festival.
There are games, music, and lots of tasty food.
Nico loves playing games
and learning new Italian words like "famiglia,"
which means family. He even tries to win
a giant stuffed pizza slice at the carnival
games!

Nico's family has a special tradition of making tomato sauce.
They pick tomatoes from Nonno's garden.
Nico helps wash the tomatoes and tries not to splash
everyone with water. Nonna and Nonno cook and jar the sauce.
This tradition, "Fare la Salsa,"
fills the house with the wonderful smell of fresh tomatoes.
The day always ends with eating fresh pasta with the new sauce,
and Nico usually ends up with sauce all over his face!

During Christmas,
Nonna bakes delicious cookies called biscotti.
Nico helps decorate them with sprinkles
and sometimes sneaks a few sprinkles into his mouth.
This tradition, "Fare i Biscotti," fills the house with sweet smells
and brings joy to everyone.

On Christmas Eve,
Nico's family celebrates with a special meal
called the Feast of the Seven Fishes, or "La Vigilia."
They eat different kinds of fish dishes to
remember their Italian roots and celebrate the holiday.
Nico learns that they aren't allowed to eat meat on this day,
but he doesn't mind because the fish dishes are so tasty!

On Christmas Day,
Nico's family has a big dinner
with roasted meats, pasta, and lots of desserts.
This tradition, "Pranzo di Natale,"
is a joyful time filled with love, laughter, and delicious food.
After dinner, the family plays cards
or a game called tombola, which is like bingo.
Nico tries to call out the numbers in a funny voice
to make everyone laugh.

On New Year's Eve,
Nico's family eats lentils and sausage.
They say it brings good luck and lots of money in the new year.
Nico giggles as they all try to eat lentils
with chopsticks for extra luck!
Everyone cheers and clinks glasses.

"Buon anno!"

Made in the USA
Las Vegas, NV
06 January 2025

15900231R00017